The Business Success of
Sandra Ortega Mera:

A Spanish Billionaire Heiress and
Influential Businesswoman Behind
a Global Fashion Powerhouse.

By

Vincenzo D. Hill

Table of Contents

Introduction

Sandra Ortega Mera is a well-known Spanish businesswoman who has made a big impact on the world. She is recognized as one of the wealthiest and most influential women in Spain. But Sandra's journey to success did not come from luck or chance; it came from hard work, a strong family background, and a clear vision of what she wanted to achieve. In this chapter, we will take a brief look at Sandra's life, the influence of her family, and how she became a powerful figure in the global business world, particularly in fashion.

Sandra was born in Spain on July 19, 1968, into a family that would later become known around the world. Her father, Amancio Ortega Gaona, is the founder of Inditex, the company behind the famous fashion brand Zara. Her mother, Rosalía Mera, was a businesswoman and philanthropist who supported many important causes. Sandra's parents worked very hard to build their business from the ground up, and their success played an important role in shaping Sandra's own values and approach to life.

Growing up, Sandra saw how her parents worked together to create a company that would become one of the largest fashion retailers in the world. She understood from an early age that business was about more than just making money; it was about creating something that could make a difference in people's lives. From her father,

Sandra learned the importance of being innovative and staying ahead of the competition. From her mother, she learned the value of helping others and supporting social causes.

Sandra's family had a strong influence on her, but they also taught her the importance of staying grounded. Despite their great wealth and success, they lived modestly and believed in maintaining a low profile. Sandra, like her parents, chose to focus on her work and keep her personal life private. She did not seek the spotlight but instead concentrated on how she could contribute to her family's business and make a difference in the world.

Sandra's path to becoming a powerful figure in business began after her mother passed away in 2013. It was at this point that Sandra inherited a portion of her mother's shares in Inditex, the company that her father had built. This inheritance made Sandra one of the wealthiest women in Spain, with a net worth of several billion dollars. However, the money and the title were not what motivated her. Sandra's true passion was to continue her family's work and make sure that the company they had built could continue to grow and adapt to the changing world.

Inditex, the parent company of Zara, is known for its unique approach to fashion. It is not just about selling clothes; it is about understanding what people want, when they want it, and how to provide it in a way that is quick and efficient. Sandra was very involved in the company's decision-making and worked to ensure that Inditex remained at the forefront of the global fashion industry. She also played a key role in managing the company's growth, helping it expand into new markets and stay competitive in an ever-changing world.

But Sandra's role in business did not stop with Inditex. She also became involved in other industries, including pharmaceuticals. Sandra invested in PharmaMar, a leading pharmaceutical company that focuses on cancer research and drug development. By diversifying her investments, Sandra showed that she was not just a businesswoman focused on fashion, but someone who cared about the future of health and science as well.

In addition to her business ventures, Sandra is also known for her philanthropic work. Her mother, Rosalía Mera, founded Fundación Paideia Galiza, an organization dedicated to helping people with disabilities. Sandra took on her mother's role and continued to support this important cause. She believed that helping others was just as important as making money and that businesses should do more than just generate profits—they should also make a positive impact on society. Through her work with Fundación Paideia Galiza, Sandra has been able to support many people in need and give back to her community.

Despite her immense wealth and success, Sandra remains humble. She does not seek attention or fame. Instead, she focuses on doing good work and making smart decisions for the companies she is involved in. She is known for being a quiet leader who prefers to work behind the scenes, letting her actions speak louder than words. Sandra's approach to business is about building long-term success, not chasing short-term gains. She understands that true success is not just measured by money but by the positive impact one can have on the world.

Sandra's family has always been a strong influence on her, but she has also created her own legacy. She has worked hard to ensure that the values of her parents are carried forward. She learned from them the importance of innovation, dedication, and giving back to society. Sandra Ortega Mera's life is a great example of how family values, hard work, and a clear vision can lead to success in the business world.

In this book, we will explore Sandra's journey in more detail. We will look at how she inherited a business empire and worked to keep it thriving. We will also see how she became involved in other industries, made wise investments, and supported important social causes. Sandra's story is not just about wealth and business; it is about how she has used her position to make a difference in the world.

Sandra Ortega Mera's journey shows that success is not just about financial gain. It is about using your resources to help others and create lasting change. Her family's influence, combined with her own dedication and vision, has helped her become one of the most powerful and respected figures in the business world today. She is a leader who has used her wealth and influence to build a better future for others, proving that true success is not just about what you achieve for yourself, but also about how you help others along the way.

This book will take you through Sandra's story, showing how she became a business powerhouse and an influential leader in the global fashion industry. It will also highlight the important lessons we can learn from her life, making it clear that success comes from hard work, a strong sense of purpose, and a commitment to helping others.

Chapter 1: Early Life and Family Influence

Sandra Ortega Mera was born on July 19, 1968, in Spain, into a family that would become one of the most influential in the world. Her father, Amancio Ortega Gaona, was the founder of Inditex, the company that owns the global fashion brand Zara. Her mother, Rosalía Mera, was also an important figure in business and social causes. Growing up in this unique environment, Sandra was exposed to the world of business at an early age, and this shaped the person she would become.

Sandra's parents were hardworking and driven. Her father, Amancio, started his journey in business at a young age, working in a clothing store. Over time, he built a clothing empire that would change the fashion industry forever. In 1985, he founded Inditex, which would later grow to become one of the largest fashion companies in the world. The flagship brand of Inditex, Zara, became known for its quick turnaround of fashion trends, offering customers the latest styles in a matter of weeks. This was a big achievement and set Inditex apart from other fashion companies.

Sandra's mother, Rosalía Mera, was also a key part of the family's business success. She helped her husband build the foundation for Inditex, and she was involved in various business ventures of her own. Rosalía had a strong interest in social causes and was passionate about helping others. She founded Fundación Paideia Galiza, a charity dedicated to helping people with disabilities, which was very important to Sandra and her family. Through her mother's example, Sandra learned the importance of helping those in need and the power of giving back to society.

Growing up in such an influential family, Sandra had a front-row seat to the world of business. She witnessed the dedication and hard work that her parents put into building their empire. Sandra's childhood was not like that of most other children; instead of focusing only on play and school, she was learning lessons in business, leadership, and responsibility. She saw how her parents made tough decisions, and how they remained focused on their goals, even in the face of challenges.

Sandra's family was not only successful in business but also grounded in strong values. Despite their wealth, they lived modestly and kept a low profile. Sandra's parents believed in staying humble and focused on their work, rather than seeking attention or fame. This approach had a big impact on Sandra. She grew up understanding that success was about more than just money—it was about making a positive difference in the world.

From a young age, Sandra learned the importance of hard work and perseverance. Her father, Amancio, was known for his strong work ethic and his commitment to making Inditex a success. He was always focused on improving his company and finding new ways to meet the needs of customers. Sandra admired her father's drive and determination, and these qualities stayed with her as she grew older.

Sandra's exposure to Inditex was a significant part of her childhood. While many children might not have been interested in their parents' businesses, Sandra was curious and engaged. She would hear about the decisions her father made, the challenges he faced, and the way he always focused on the future. Sandra understood early on that business was not just about making money, but about being innovative and staying ahead of the competition. Her family's work was not just about creating a successful company—it was about changing the way people shopped and interacted with fashion.

Her exposure to business didn't stop with Zara. Sandra learned the importance of diversification from her family. Inditex was not the only source of their success; they also invested in other industries, including pharmaceuticals. Sandra's mother, Rosalía, made sure to involve her in their broader business activities, teaching her that it was important to invest wisely and to think beyond the company's core industry. This early lesson in business diversification would help Sandra later on when she became involved in other companies outside of Inditex, like PharmaMar, a pharmaceutical company focused on cancer research and drug development.

In addition to her parents' business influence, Sandra was also shaped by their values. Both of her parents were dedicated to helping others, and they taught Sandra that giving back was an essential part of success. Rosalía's work with Fundación Paideia Galiza showed Sandra the importance of social responsibility. Through this foundation, Sandra learned that business success could be used as a tool to support causes that make a real difference in people's lives. Her mother's example made Sandra want to find ways to give back to society, and this would become an important part of her life and career later on.

Sandra's upbringing also gave her a strong sense of responsibility. As the daughter of two very successful individuals, Sandra understood that the family's legacy was something she would eventually need to carry on. She knew that inheriting a portion of her mother's shares in Inditex after Rosalía's death in 2013 was not just about receiving wealth—it was about continuing the vision that her parents had worked so hard to build. Sandra took this responsibility seriously, and it would guide her decisions in the years to come.

Sandra's family's influence was not limited to business lessons alone. She was also taught the value of maintaining a private life. Unlike many wealthy individuals who are often in the public eye, Sandra and her family preferred to stay out of the spotlight. They focused on their work, not on seeking fame. Sandra admired this approach and chose to live a life of humility, despite the wealth and power she inherited. This value of privacy would help her maintain a low profile throughout her career, focusing on the work itself rather than the attention it might bring.

In many ways, Sandra Ortega Mera's childhood was a preparation for the challenges and responsibilities she would face later in life. Growing up in a family that built a global fashion empire taught her the importance of hard work, innovation, and giving back. Her parents' commitment to their business and their social causes had a profound impact on Sandra's values and interests. She learned not only how to be a business leader but also how to be a responsible and humble individual. These lessons would shape her into the powerful and influential figure she would become in the global business world.

Sandra's early life was filled with lessons that laid the foundation for her future. Her parents' business achievements and their values shaped her approach to work and life. She understood the importance of innovation, responsibility, and helping others. These lessons would stay with her as she became a key figure in the world of fashion and business. Sandra Ortega Mera's family background and early experiences helped her grow into the successful businesswoman she is today.

Chapter 2: Education and Personal Growth

Sandra Ortega Mera's education and personal growth played an important role in shaping her into the businesswoman she is today. Though she grew up in a family famous for its business success, Sandra took a different path when it came to her academic journey. Rather than immediately jumping into the family business, she chose to study psychology, a decision that would influence her approach to business and leadership later in life.

Sandra's early education in Spain provided a solid foundation, but it was her time in higher education that would shape her future path. Sandra decided to attend the University of A Coruña, where she pursued a degree in psychology. This choice may seem unusual given her family's strong ties to the business world, but it was a decision rooted in Sandra's desire for personal growth and understanding. She didn't just want to learn about business; she wanted to understand people, behavior, and the ways in which individuals make decisions.

Psychology provided Sandra with valuable insights into the human mind, emotions, and motivations. She was particularly interested in understanding how individuals react to various situations and how those reactions can shape business decisions. Psychology also helped her understand the importance of effective communication and empathy, both of which would be essential as she took on leadership roles in her family's businesses.

During her studies, Sandra focused on learning how to listen to people, understand their needs, and make decisions that were not only logical but also considerate of the people involved. These skills would become vital when she began working in her family's companies, where understanding employees, customers, and partners was key to success. Sandra's education helped her develop a deep understanding of human behavior, which gave her an edge when it came to managing relationships and building trust.

In addition to her academic education, Sandra's personal growth was shaped by her experiences outside the classroom. Sandra was determined to gain a well-rounded perspective on the world, so she spent time traveling, meeting new people, and learning about different cultures. These experiences helped Sandra expand her worldview and gain a deeper appreciation for the diversity of thought, opinion, and creativity that exists in the world. This exposure to different ways of thinking would influence her approach to business, encouraging her to consider new ideas and perspectives when making decisions.

Sandra's choice to study psychology also reflected her desire to carve out her own identity outside of her father's legacy. She didn't want to simply follow in her family's footsteps; she wanted to develop her own skills, interests, and passions. By choosing psychology, Sandra showed that she valued intellectual curiosity and personal development over simply taking the easy route of stepping directly into the family business.

While studying psychology, Sandra also began to gain a better understanding of leadership. She realized that being a leader wasn't just about making decisions or having authority. It was about inspiring others, listening to their concerns, and helping them achieve their full potential. She understood that a good leader needed to create an environment where people felt respected and valued, and this was something she learned during her time in school.

At the same time, Sandra was developing a strong sense of responsibility. She knew that one day she would be taking on a significant role in her family's businesses, and she wanted to be ready for that. Sandra's academic pursuits were not just about gaining knowledge; they were about preparing herself to be an effective and compassionate leader who could carry on her family's legacy while also making her own mark in the business world.

Her education in psychology also taught her about the power of emotional intelligence. Sandra learned that being able to recognize, understand, and manage emotions—both her own and those of others—was a crucial skill in business. Emotional intelligence is essential for building strong relationships, motivating teams, and resolving conflicts. Sandra's ability to connect with people on a deeper emotional level would later prove to be one of her greatest strengths as she navigated the challenges of managing her family's vast business empire.

Sandra's time in university also played a key role in shaping her approach to work-life balance. Unlike many high-powered executives, Sandra believed in the importance of taking time for herself and maintaining personal well-being. She realized that in order to be an effective leader, she needed to take care of her own mental and emotional health. This mindset helped her avoid burnout and stay focused on her long-term goals.

In addition to her education, Sandra's personal growth was influenced by the strong family values that were instilled in her from a young age. She learned the importance of humility, responsibility, and empathy, and these values would guide her throughout her life and career. Sandra's parents, Amancio and Rosalía, taught her the importance of staying grounded and not letting success or wealth define who she was as a person. This sense of humility was something that Sandra carried with her into adulthood, and it shaped her approach to both business and life.

Sandra's personal growth wasn't just about intellectual development; it was also about emotional maturity. As she navigated her way through the challenges of education and growing up in a prominent family, she learned how to cope with the pressures and expectations that came with her family's legacy. Sandra knew that she had big shoes to fill, but rather than feeling burdened by this, she used it as motivation to grow into a leader who could contribute meaningfully to her family's success.

By the time Sandra completed her studies, she had become a well-rounded individual with a deep understanding of psychology, leadership, and the human condition. These skills would serve her well as she took on more responsibility in her family's businesses, particularly in the global fashion empire that her father had built. Sandra's ability to understand people and make thoughtful, compassionate decisions set her apart from many others in the business world.

Sandra's education and personal growth laid the foundation for her success in the world of business. Her academic choice to study psychology was more than just an intellectual pursuit—it was an investment in her future as a compassionate, effective, and innovative leader. The skills she developed during her education, combined with her strong family values, helped Sandra grow into the powerful businesswoman she would become. As Sandra took on new challenges and responsibilities in her family's businesses, she was well-prepared to face the complexities of the business world and navigate the opportunities and obstacles that lay ahead.

Chapter 3: Inheriting a Fashion Empire

In 2013, Sandra Ortega Mera faced a turning point in her life that would change everything. It was the year her mother, Rosalía Mera, passed away. With her mother's death, Sandra inherited a share in Inditex, the global fashion giant that her father, Amancio Ortega, had built. This moment marked the beginning of Sandra's deeper involvement in the family business. It also brought with it a tremendous sense of responsibility and a realization of the weight of the legacy she was now a part of.

Inditex, the company Sandra inherited a stake in, is one of the world's largest fashion retailers, with well-known brands like Zara, Massimo Dutti, and Pull&Bear under its umbrella. The company has revolutionized the fashion industry with its fast-fashion model, creating stylish clothing and getting it into stores faster than many competitors. Sandra's inheritance was not just about money—it was about joining a family legacy that had reshaped the global fashion landscape.

Sandra's reaction to inheriting part of Inditex was one of deep reflection. It was a significant moment in her life, and she understood the responsibilities that came with it. While her mother had been involved in the early stages of the business, especially with her support for the development of Zara, it was her father, Amancio, who was more closely associated with Inditex's rapid growth. Sandra had always been involved with the family business, but now, with this inheritance, her role was becoming much more significant. She had to decide how to navigate her place within such a large, successful empire.

The responsibility of inheriting a share in Inditex was heavy for Sandra. It wasn't just about being a wealthy heir; it was about ensuring that the company continued to thrive. She knew that the decisions she made in the future would impact not only her family but also the thousands of employees working for the company and the millions of customers who relied on its products. The pressure was immense, but Sandra had grown up with the values of responsibility, humility, and hard work that her parents had instilled in her. These values would guide her as she stepped into a more prominent role in the family business.

Sandra was not new to the world of business. She had already been learning about the company, especially through her education and early involvement in the family's ventures. However, after her mother's passing, Sandra had to fully embrace her role in the company. She began attending meetings, getting more involved with strategic decisions, and understanding how the various departments of Inditex operated. She knew that in order to honor her family's legacy, she needed to learn as much as possible about the business and its inner workings.

One of the first things Sandra did after inheriting the share in Inditex was to focus on building strong relationships with the people who worked at all levels of the company. She recognized that her success in the business world would depend not only on her decision-making skills but also on her ability to connect with others. Sandra had always been a people-oriented individual, and she used her skills in psychology to understand the needs, desires, and concerns of employees and business partners. She wanted to be a leader who was not just about the bottom line, but who truly cared about the people who contributed to the company's success.

Sandra's involvement in Inditex wasn't just about making money—it was about continuing the vision her parents had set. She took the task of preserving the company's values seriously. Inditex was founded on principles like innovation, fast adaptation to market trends, and a commitment to quality. Sandra understood the importance of maintaining these values as the company continued to grow, especially as it expanded into new markets around the world. She knew that in order to keep the company's success going, it would be essential to stay true to its roots while also looking for new opportunities for growth.

While Sandra was stepping into a more visible role within the family business, she didn't want to rely solely on the legacy of her parents. She was determined to bring her own perspective to the company. Sandra began thinking about how Inditex could modernize further, particularly in its approach to sustainability and digital transformation. She saw the increasing importance of technology in the fashion industry and understood that the future of fashion would be shaped by innovations in e-commerce, supply chains, and the integration of artificial intelligence. This insight would become a central part of her strategy for the company moving forward.

One of the challenges Sandra faced after inheriting the family's wealth and business was the need to balance her role as a shareholder with the responsibilities of leading the company. In many family-owned businesses, the line between ownership and management can become blurry, and this was something Sandra had to navigate. While she now had a greater influence in the company's decisions, she was careful not to overshadow the other leaders within Inditex who had years of experience. Sandra's approach was one of collaboration and respect, working alongside the management team to ensure that the company continued to innovate and lead the global fashion industry.

Sandra also took the opportunity to invest in areas that were important to her, both personally and professionally. She was particularly passionate about fashion sustainability and how Inditex could reduce its environmental impact. Sandra believed that fashion could be both stylish and responsible, and she worked to integrate more sustainable practices into the company's operations. Whether it was sourcing eco-friendly materials, reducing waste, or improving working conditions in factories, Sandra saw sustainability as a critical area where Inditex could continue to lead the way.

In addition to her work in fashion, Sandra's philanthropic activities also became a more prominent part of her legacy. She used her influence and resources to support causes that were important to her, including initiatives that promoted education, healthcare, and social equality. Sandra's approach to philanthropy was similar to her approach to business: thoughtful, strategic, and focused on making a lasting impact.

Over time, Sandra began to embrace her role as the heir to Inditex more fully. She worked to gain the trust of her family, the company's management, and the employees. Her leadership style was grounded in humility, empathy, and a commitment to preserving the family's values while pushing the company into the future. As she continued to grow into her role, Sandra realized that her inheritance was not just a gift—it was an opportunity to make a meaningful impact on the business world and the lives of those around her.

Inheriting a share in Inditex in 2013 was a pivotal moment for Sandra Ortega Mera. It marked the beginning of a new chapter in her life, one filled with great responsibility, challenges, and opportunities. Sandra's response to this inheritance was a combination of reflection, hard work, and determination. With the lessons she had learned from her family, her education, and her own personal experiences, Sandra was ready to step into her role in the family business and ensure that Inditex would continue to be a global leader in fashion for years to come.

Chapter 4: Inditex and the Global Impact of Zara

Inditex is one of the most successful fashion companies in the world, and Zara is its most well-known brand. The company, founded by Amancio Ortega and Rosalía Mera, has revolutionized the way people shop for clothes. Sandra Ortega Mera, as part of the family, has continued to play an important role in the company's success. This chapter looks at how Inditex operates, what makes Zara so successful, and the global impact it has had on the fashion industry.

How Inditex Works

Inditex is a huge company with many different brands, but Zara is the most famous. Other brands in the Inditex group include Massimo Dutti, Pull&Bear, Stradivarius, and Bershka. These brands all offer stylish clothing, but each has its own unique focus. For example, Zara is known for trendy, high-fashion pieces, while Massimo Dutti has a more classic, professional style.

What makes Inditex unique is its business model. One of the main reasons for its success is how quickly it can get new designs into stores. Most fashion companies take months to design and produce clothes, but Zara is different. It can take Zara as little as two weeks to design, produce, and deliver new clothes to stores. This quick turnaround is a key reason why Zara is able to stay ahead of fashion trends and keep customers coming back for more.

Sandra Ortega Mera, now deeply involved in the business, helps ensure that Inditex's operations continue smoothly. She is responsible for helping guide the company's strategies, making sure that Zara and other brands grow and stay competitive in a fast-changing fashion world. Sandra's background in psychology has also played a role in how she approaches business. She understands people and knows how to create environments where both employees and customers feel valued.

The Unique Business Strategies of Zara

Zara's ability to get new clothes to stores quickly is part of its success, but there are other strategies that make the brand stand out. One of the key strategies Zara uses is a system called "fast fashion." This means that Zara doesn't just follow trends; it creates and adapts new styles quickly to meet customer demand. Instead of designing clothes months in advance, Zara's designers watch what's happening in fashion and quickly create new designs that reflect what people are looking for.

Zara also keeps production close to home. While many fashion brands manufacture clothes in faraway countries, Zara keeps many of its factories in Europe, close to its headquarters in Spain. This allows the company to respond quickly to changes in demand and avoid long shipping times. If a design becomes popular, Zara can make more quickly and ship it to stores around the world in just a few weeks.

Another important part of Zara's business strategy is its focus on customer feedback. Zara listens closely to its customers. The company's stores are designed to gather feedback on what people like and don't like. If something is selling well, Zara orders more of it. If something is not selling, it can be pulled from the shelves almost immediately. This is a big part of why Zara stores are constantly changing their inventory. Customers never know exactly what they will find, which makes shopping at Zara exciting.

Zara also uses a system called "just in time" inventory. This means that Zara doesn't produce too many clothes at once. Instead, it makes just enough to meet customer demand. This helps avoid the waste that can happen when clothes go unsold. By being more efficient, Zara helps reduce costs, and that makes it easier to offer trendy clothing at affordable prices.

Zara's Global Expansion

Zara's business strategies have helped it become one of the largest and most well-known fashion retailers in the world. What started as a small store in Spain in

1975 is now a global brand with thousands of stores in countries around the world. Sandra Ortega Mera, as part of the family, has helped the brand continue its global expansion.

One of the reasons Zara has been so successful worldwide is its ability to adapt to different markets. Whether in Europe, the United States, or Asia, Zara designs clothing that appeals to the tastes of local customers. For example, while European customers may like a more classic, tailored look, Asian customers may prefer more casual or brightly colored styles. Zara pays attention to these preferences and adapts its clothing collections accordingly.

Zara's global presence is also supported by its online store. The brand has embraced the rise of e-commerce and uses it as another way to connect with customers. Online shopping has become increasingly popular, and Zara's ability to provide the latest trends both in stores and online has helped it stay relevant to customers around the world.

Zara has also embraced social media as part of its marketing strategy. Platforms like Instagram, Facebook, and Twitter allow the brand to reach a younger, tech-savvy audience who are always looking for the latest fashion. Zara often uses social media to showcase new collections and let customers know what's coming next. This direct connection with customers has been a powerful tool in building Zara's global influence.

The Influence of Zara in the Fashion Industry

Zara's influence on the fashion industry is undeniable. It has changed the way people think about shopping for clothes. Before Zara's rise, fashion brands would often release collections once or twice a year, with long lead times for production. But Zara's fast fashion model has changed that. Now, customers expect to see new styles in stores every few weeks. Zara has made fashion more accessible, and more people around the world are able to enjoy high-quality, trendy clothing at affordable prices.

Zara has also influenced other brands. Many companies have tried to replicate Zara's success by adopting similar fast fashion strategies. Some have even tried to copy Zara's business model of producing clothing quickly and efficiently. However, Zara's ability to stay ahead of trends and provide the latest designs remains one of the key reasons it continues to lead the market.

Sandra Ortega Mera's role in Zara's success is not just about the money she inherited. It is also about her understanding of the importance of innovation, sustainability, and customer satisfaction. She has played an active role in shaping the direction of the company, making sure that Zara remains at the forefront of the fashion world.

Sustainability and Future Growth

As Zara continues to grow, Sandra Ortega Mera has also focused on the importance of sustainability. The fashion industry has faced increasing scrutiny for its environmental impact, and Zara has made strides to reduce its carbon footprint. The company has started using more eco-friendly materials, improving its production processes, and working to reduce waste. Sandra's leadership has pushed the company to make fashion that is not only stylish but also responsible.

Looking to the future, Zara will continue to be a major player in the global fashion industry. With Sandra Ortega Mera's guidance, the company will likely keep expanding into new markets and adapting to changing customer needs. Whether through its online presence, its fast-fashion model, or its commitment to sustainability, Zara will remain a brand that millions of people around the world rely on for the latest trends.

In conclusion, Zara's success and its global impact on the fashion industry cannot be overstated. With innovative business strategies, a focus on customer satisfaction, and a commitment to sustainability, Zara has become a global powerhouse in the fashion world. Sandra Ortega Mera, as part of the Ortega family, plays an important role in guiding the company's future, ensuring that it continues to lead the way in the ever-changing world of fashion.

Chapter 5: Building a Role in Business

Sandra Ortega Mera is often known as the daughter of Amancio Ortega, the founder of Inditex, but her story goes far beyond just being an heiress. In fact, she has worked hard to build her own identity in the business world. Sandra has focused on creating value, working on projects that matter to her, and shaping her role with a commitment to responsible growth. This chapter looks at how Sandra developed her business career and the steps she took to create a positive impact in both her company and the wider business community.

Moving Beyond the Title of Heiress

Sandra Ortega Mera's life was shaped by her family's business. From a young age, she was exposed to the world of fashion and business through her parents' work. However, Sandra did not want to simply rely on her family's wealth and legacy. She knew that to make a real impact, she needed to carve out her own role and bring her own ideas into the business world.

Growing up, Sandra observed how her father worked tirelessly to build Inditex into one of the largest fashion companies in the world. While she respected his success, Sandra realized that she wanted to create her own path, separate from being just an heir to a business empire. She did not take her position for granted. Instead, she dedicated herself to learning about business and exploring how she could add value in her own way.

Sandra began her journey by working on different projects within the family business. She took time to understand how Inditex operated, focusing on the core values that had made the company successful, such as innovation, efficiency, and responsiveness to customer needs. Sandra also paid close attention to the company's efforts to grow sustainably, recognizing that the future of business would depend on responsible practices.

Focus on Creating Value

One of Sandra's key goals was to create value through her work. She did not want to simply manage wealth; she wanted to contribute to the world in a way that was meaningful and long-lasting. Sandra understood that business is not just about making money—it's also about solving problems and improving people's lives.

Sandra's first step was to focus on the areas of business where she felt she could make a difference. She became particularly interested in the idea of social responsibility in business. While her family's company, Inditex, had already started to address environmental concerns, Sandra pushed for even more sustainable practices. She began looking for ways to make the company more eco-friendly and reduce its carbon footprint.

Sandra also worked to ensure that the company's supply chain was transparent. She believed that businesses should be accountable for the way they operate, especially when it comes to sourcing materials and treating workers fairly. Sandra used her position to encourage Inditex to invest more in ethical practices, ensuring that the company's clothing was made in ways that were good for both people and the planet.

Sandra's dedication to creating value went beyond just her family business. She was also involved in several other ventures that reflected her personal interests and values.

For example, Sandra worked on projects related to education, aiming to improve access to quality education for young people. This was another way she wanted to give back to society, using her position to make a difference in areas outside of fashion.

Taking on Leadership Roles

Sandra's journey in business was not just about making decisions within Inditex. She also wanted to develop as a leader in her own right. As part of her efforts to step out of her father's shadow, Sandra began taking on more visible roles in the company. She became actively involved in key projects and decision-making processes, always with a focus on growth that was responsible and ethical.

She took a strong interest in the company's future, particularly how Inditex could continue to grow while maintaining its commitment to sustainability. Sandra believed that for businesses to succeed in the long term, they needed to adapt to changing environmental and social demands. She was a strong advocate for integrating these values into the company's overall strategy, ensuring that business growth did not come at the cost of the planet or society.

As part of her leadership development, Sandra also focused on improving her skills in areas like finance, management, and innovation. While she had a solid foundation thanks to her upbringing, she understood that the business world was constantly changing. Sandra knew that to be an effective leader, she needed to keep learning and adapting. This is why she took courses and sought advice from experts in various fields. She didn't just rely on her family name; she worked hard to build the skills and knowledge necessary to lead.

Sandra's leadership style became defined by her commitment to clear communication, teamwork, and continuous improvement. She valued input from others and created an environment where employees could share ideas. Sandra believed that the best ideas come from many voices, and she worked to make sure that people felt heard and respected in the company.

Shaping Her Business Identity

Sandra Ortega Mera's business identity is deeply rooted in her values of responsibility, sustainability, and innovation. She didn't just want to carry on her family's legacy—she wanted to shape it in a way that aligned with her own vision for the future. Her work within Inditex, as well as her personal projects, all reflect a commitment to making the world a better place.

One of the ways Sandra shaped her business identity was by pushing for transparency in business practices. She was a strong believer that companies should be open about where they source their materials and how they treat their workers. This transparency was important not only for maintaining customer trust but also for creating a culture of accountability within the company.

In addition to her work in sustainability, Sandra also played an important role in the company's digital transformation. As the world of retail began to shift towards online shopping, Sandra helped steer Inditex toward new digital technologies that would improve the customer experience. She understood that staying competitive meant embracing change and looking for innovative ways to reach customers.

Sandra also believed that business should be a force for good. She used her position to advocate for initiatives that would improve the quality of life for people in communities where Inditex operated. Whether through supporting local charities or helping improve workers' conditions in factories, Sandra worked to ensure that the business could create positive impacts far beyond the fashion world.

Responsible Growth and Long-Term Success

One of Sandra Ortega Mera's most important goals in business has been responsible growth. While many companies are focused on short-term profits, Sandra has always believed in building businesses that can succeed over the long run. She understands that businesses must evolve to stay relevant, but they must also take care of the planet and its people.

Sandra has worked to ensure that Inditex's growth is sustainable, both environmentally and socially. She has made sure that the company invests in green technologies, reduces waste, and works with suppliers who share similar values. In doing so, Sandra has helped create a business model that focuses not just on making money but also on improving the world for future generations.

By focusing on responsible growth, Sandra has positioned herself as a leader who cares deeply about the impact her business has on the world. She understands that true success in business is not only about numbers and profits but also about creating a legacy of positive change. Through her work, Sandra Ortega Mera continues to build a role in business that reflects her commitment to responsibility, sustainability, and innovation.

In conclusion, Sandra Ortega Mera has successfully developed her own identity as a business leader. She has done this by focusing on creating value, taking on leadership roles, and making responsible decisions that help her family's business grow in a sustainable and ethical way. Sandra's business journey shows that success is not just about inheriting wealth—it's about working hard, making a difference, and building something that will have a positive impact for years to come.

Chapter 6: Expanding into Pharmaceuticals

Sandra Ortega Mera is known for her work in the fashion industry, but she has also made a big impact in another area: healthcare. Through her investments in PharmaMar, a leading pharmaceutical company, Sandra has shown a strong interest in medical innovation. This chapter will explore why Sandra decided to invest in the pharmaceutical field, why she believes it is important, and what she hopes to achieve through her contributions.

Understanding PharmaMar

PharmaMar is a company focused on developing innovative medicines, especially those that target cancer. It is known for its work in discovering new drugs from natural sources like marine life. The company believes that nature holds many secrets that can help fight diseases. PharmaMar uses advanced science to turn these natural resources into life-saving treatments.

Sandra first became interested in PharmaMar because of its cutting-edge research and its focus on using nature to develop medicines. She was impressed by the company's efforts to discover new treatments for difficult-to-treat diseases, especially cancer. Sandra has always cared about improving people's lives, and she saw PharmaMar as a way to contribute to this mission in a very meaningful way.

The Decision to Invest in Healthcare

Sandra's decision to invest in PharmaMar was not random. She had always believed in the power of business to make a positive impact on society. While her family's company, Inditex, focused on fashion, Sandra wanted to expand her influence in a way that could help people's health. By investing in PharmaMar, Sandra entered a field where the stakes are high and the potential to help others is immense.

One of the reasons Sandra chose to invest in PharmaMar is because she saw healthcare as a way to make a direct difference in people's lives. Many people around the world suffer from serious illnesses like cancer, and the need for better treatments is constant. Sandra believed that supporting companies like PharmaMar could help bring new solutions to these problems. She felt it was important to support scientific research that could lead to life-saving discoveries.

In addition to her personal interest in healthcare, Sandra also recognized the financial potential of investing in the pharmaceutical industry. Pharmaceuticals are one of the largest and most important industries in the world, and companies like PharmaMar are always looking for new investors to help fund their research and development. By supporting PharmaMar,

Sandra could help the company grow, while also benefiting from the financial returns of her investment.

Why Healthcare Matters to Sandra

Sandra Ortega Mera's interest in healthcare goes beyond just making a profit. She truly cares about the impact that medical innovation can have on the world. In many ways, her decision to support PharmaMar reflects her belief that business should be a force for good.

Healthcare is a critical issue for millions of people worldwide. Many diseases, especially cancers, are difficult to treat, and finding new treatments is a long and expensive process. Sandra recognized that by investing in companies focused on medical research, she could help bring new drugs and therapies to market that could save lives.

For Sandra, healthcare is about improving the quality of life for people who are suffering from serious illnesses. She knows that diseases like cancer are not just medical issues—they are personal and emotional challenges for patients and their families. By supporting the development of new treatments, Sandra hopes to make a difference for people who are fighting these difficult battles.

Sandra's Vision for Medical Innovation

Sandra Ortega Mera's vision for her investments in PharmaMar goes beyond simply helping the company succeed. She wants to be part of something bigger: a movement toward better healthcare and more effective treatments. Through her support, Sandra hopes to play a role in accelerating the development of new therapies that can change the lives of people facing serious illnesses.

One of Sandra's goals is to help PharmaMar continue its groundbreaking research into cancer treatments. Cancer remains one of the leading causes of death worldwide, and Sandra believes that finding better treatments is one of the most important challenges of our time. By investing in PharmaMar, Sandra hopes to ensure that the company can continue its important work of developing innovative drugs that target cancer cells in new and more effective ways.

Sandra also supports PharmaMar's focus on using natural resources, like marine life, in its research. Many of the company's most promising drugs come from the ocean, where unique organisms produce powerful compounds that can be used to fight diseases. Sandra believes that by harnessing the power of nature, companies like PharmaMar can discover new treatments that might not be found through traditional methods. This innovative approach to medicine is something Sandra is passionate about supporting.

Challenges in the Pharmaceutical Industry

The pharmaceutical industry is not without its challenges. Developing new drugs is a complex, expensive, and time-consuming process. It can take years or even decades to bring a new drug from the lab to the patient, and not every drug makes it through the process. In addition, the healthcare industry is highly regulated, which can make it difficult for companies to navigate the legal and safety requirements for new medicines.

Despite these challenges, Sandra Ortega Mera remains committed to supporting PharmaMar and its mission. She understands that the road to medical innovation is not always smooth, but she is confident that the rewards—better health for people around the world—are worth the effort. Sandra is willing to be patient and persistent, knowing that the investments made today could lead to breakthroughs in the future.

Making a Difference Through Investment

Sandra's investments in PharmaMar are not just financial—they are part of her broader goal of making a difference in the world. By supporting companies that focus on medical research and innovation, Sandra is helping to fund the development of life-saving treatments.

She is also helping to raise awareness about the importance of investing in healthcare. As one of the key investors in PharmaMar,

Sandra's involvement in the company sends a strong message to others in the business world: healthcare is a worthy investment. Companies that focus on improving health and finding new treatments deserve the support of investors who believe in their mission.

Sandra has always believed that business can have a positive impact on society. Her work in the pharmaceutical industry is an example of how business leaders can use their resources to support causes that matter. By investing in PharmaMar, Sandra is not only helping to fund the development of new treatments, but she is also contributing to the broader effort to improve healthcare around the world.

The Future of Sandra's Healthcare Investments

Sandra Ortega Mera's investments in PharmaMar are just the beginning of her journey in the healthcare industry. She is committed to supporting medical research and innovation, and she plans to continue her involvement in the pharmaceutical field in the years to come.

Through her investments, Sandra hopes to be part of a movement that brings better health to people all over the world. By supporting companies like PharmaMar, she is helping to create a future where new treatments are available to those who need them most. Sandra's contributions to the healthcare industry are a testament to her belief that business can be a powerful force for good in the world.

In conclusion, Sandra Ortega Mera's decision to invest in PharmaMar reflects her commitment to making a positive impact on the world. Through her support of medical innovation, Sandra is helping to bring new treatments to market that can save lives and improve health. Her investments are about more than just financial returns—they are about making a difference for people facing serious illnesses. Sandra's work in healthcare shows that business leaders have the power to create meaningful change, and that by investing in medical research, we can all help build a healthier future.

Chapter 7: Philanthropy and Social Responsibility

Sandra Ortega Mera is not just known for her work in business and her investments in companies like Zara and PharmaMar. She is also deeply involved in helping others through her charitable work. One of her most important contributions is through the Fundación Paideia Galiza, an organization dedicated to supporting people with disabilities and helping them lead fulfilling lives. This chapter will explore Sandra's philanthropic efforts, focusing on how she has used her resources to make a positive difference in society.

The Mission of Fundación Paideia Galiza

Fundación Paideia Galiza is an organization that Sandra Ortega Mera is closely connected to. The foundation's primary mission is to support people with disabilities, ensuring they have the resources, opportunities, and support they need to live their lives with dignity and independence. The foundation works to create an inclusive society where everyone, regardless of their physical or mental challenges, can participate fully in life.

Sandra's involvement with Fundación Paideia Galiza is personal. She has always believed that helping those who are disadvantaged or marginalized is one of the most important responsibilities a person can have. By supporting Fundación Paideia Galiza, Sandra has made it her goal to help improve the quality of life for people with disabilities, whether through education, training, or social programs that promote inclusion.

One of the foundation's main initiatives is offering vocational training to people with disabilities. This training helps them develop skills that are useful in the workplace, giving them a chance to secure jobs and become financially independent. The foundation believes that everyone deserves a chance to work and contribute to society, and it provides the necessary support to make that possible.

Sandra's Commitment to Social Causes

Sandra Ortega Mera's commitment to social responsibility goes beyond just helping people with disabilities. She believes that businesses and individuals have a duty to give back to society. Sandra's efforts reflect her belief that success should be measured not just by financial achievements, but by the positive impact one can have on the community.

Through her charitable work, Sandra has shown that she is dedicated to creating a more inclusive and equal society. She is passionate about helping those who face difficulties in life, whether due to disabilities or other social challenges. Her work with Fundación Paideia Galiza is a testament to her belief that everyone deserves equal opportunities, regardless of their circumstances.

Sandra's involvement in social causes also includes support for education, healthcare, and cultural projects. She understands that social change often starts with providing people with the tools they need to succeed. That is why she focuses her efforts on initiatives that can create long-lasting, positive change in society. For Sandra, philanthropy is not just about giving money—it is about making a real difference in people's lives.

Helping People with Disabilities Lead
Independent Lives

Sandra Ortega Mera's support for people
with disabilities is at the heart of her
philanthropic work. Through Fundación
Paideia Galiza, she has helped create
programs that offer both emotional and
practical support to individuals with
disabilities. This includes providing access
to education, healthcare, and job training, as
well as promoting awareness about the
importance of inclusion.

One of the main goals of Fundación Paideia
Galiza is to help people with disabilities live
independent lives. This means giving them
the skills, education, and opportunities they
need to take care of themselves and

contribute to society. For example, the foundation works to ensure that people with disabilities have access to job opportunities, so they can support themselves financially. It also helps provide assistance in areas like housing, transportation, and social activities, making it easier for people with disabilities to live fulfilling and active lives.

Sandra has always believed in the power of education to change lives, which is why her foundation focuses on providing education and training to people with disabilities. By offering specialized courses and vocational training, Fundación Paideia Galiza gives people the tools they need to succeed in the workplace. This is important because, often, people with disabilities face challenges when it comes to finding a job, but through education and training, they can prove their abilities and gain confidence.

Creating Awareness about Disability Inclusion

Another key aspect of Sandra Ortega Mera's philanthropic work is raising awareness about the needs of people with disabilities. Many people still have misconceptions or lack understanding of the challenges faced by individuals with disabilities. Sandra believes that creating awareness is an essential part of creating a more inclusive society. She has used her platform to encourage people to think differently about disabilities and to see the abilities, rather than just the limitations, of those affected by them.

Sandra's work with Fundación Paideia Galiza focuses on educating the public about the importance of inclusion and equal opportunities. The foundation helps change attitudes by showing the many ways in which people with disabilities can contribute to society. Through social programs, educational initiatives, and partnerships with other organizations, Sandra has worked hard to shift the way people view disability and to encourage greater acceptance and understanding.

One way Sandra has helped raise awareness is by promoting the idea of accessibility. Ensuring that public spaces, workplaces, and schools are accessible to everyone, regardless of their physical or mental abilities, is crucial. Sandra has been an advocate for changes in public policy and has worked with organizations to make sure that people with disabilities have the same opportunities as anyone else.

The Importance of Long-Term Impact

Sandra Ortega Mera is committed to creating lasting change. She believes that philanthropy should not be about short-term solutions, but about making a long-term difference in the lives of those who need help. Through Fundación Paideia Galiza, Sandra is focused on creating programs that will have a lasting impact on the lives of people with disabilities.

For example, the foundation not only helps individuals with disabilities find jobs and live independently, but it also works to change the systems and policies that affect them. By advocating for better healthcare, education, and workplace practices, Fundación Paideia Galiza is working to create a society where people with disabilities have the same opportunities as everyone else. Sandra's efforts are aimed at removing the barriers that prevent people with disabilities from fully participating in society, whether those barriers are physical, social, or financial.

Sandra understands that true social responsibility involves making a real, lasting difference. That is why she is focused on sustainable projects that will continue to benefit people with disabilities for many years to come. She believes in supporting programs that empower individuals to take charge of their own futures and that create a more just and inclusive society.

Encouraging Other Business Leaders to Give Back

Sandra Ortega Mera's philanthropic work also serves as an example to other business leaders. She believes that successful individuals and companies have a responsibility to give back to society. Through her efforts, Sandra encourages others to consider how they can contribute to social causes and make a difference in their own communities.

By focusing on social responsibility and philanthropy, Sandra hopes to inspire others to take action and use their resources for good. She believes that businesses, especially those with significant financial success, have the ability to create positive change in society. Through her charitable work, Sandra sets an example of how business leaders can use their influence to help others.

Conclusion

Sandra Ortega Mera's dedication to philanthropy and social responsibility is an important part of her legacy. Through Fundación Paideia Galiza, she has worked tirelessly to improve the lives of people with disabilities and to create a more inclusive society. Sandra's commitment to social causes reflects her belief that businesses and individuals have a duty to help others, and her work is a testament to the power of philanthropy to make lasting change. Sandra's efforts to raise awareness, support education, and promote inclusion have had a profound impact on many lives, and her dedication to helping others will continue to inspire future generations.

Chapter 8: Recognition and Influence

Sandra Ortega Mera has made a significant impact in both the business world and the charity sector. Her work has not gone unnoticed, and she has received many awards and honors that recognize her achievements. This chapter explores the recognition Sandra has received for her work, the influence she has had in Spain and beyond, and how her success serves as an inspiration to other women in business.

Awards and Recognition in Business

Sandra Ortega Mera's journey in business began when she inherited a share of the multinational company Inditex after the passing of her mother in 2013. As a shareholder and an influential member of the family, Sandra quickly gained attention for her leadership and business acumen. While she chose not to be in the public eye as much as her family members, her work in managing and supporting Inditex, as well as her business investments, was noticed by the industry.

Sandra's achievements were recognized by several prestigious organizations. One of the most notable awards she received was for her contribution to the Spanish business community. The Spanish government and various business groups acknowledged her leadership skills and the success of her endeavors. Sandra's quiet yet powerful approach to business set her apart from others in the industry. She focused on sustainable growth, social responsibility, and ethical investment, which aligned her work with the growing demand for businesses to contribute positively to society.

Sandra's impact wasn't limited to Spain. She became known internationally for her role in the success of Inditex and her dedication to responsible business practices. Her involvement with other companies, such as her investments in PharmaMar and her support for social causes, further raised her profile globally. Sandra's thoughtful and effective leadership brought her recognition as a respected business figure who understood the importance of balancing financial success with social responsibility.

Recognition for Charitable Efforts

In addition to her success in business, Sandra Ortega Mera has also been recognized for her philanthropic work. Through Fundación Paideia Galiza, which she has supported and grown, Sandra has made a positive impact on the lives of many people with disabilities. Her commitment to social causes has garnered her recognition from various organizations focused on disability rights and social inclusion.

Sandra's charitable work was honored with awards that acknowledged her dedication to improving society. The Fundación Paideia

Galiza's efforts, with Sandra's backing, helped to change the way people with disabilities are treated in Spain. The foundation worked to increase accessibility, promote inclusion, and provide training and job opportunities for individuals with disabilities. Sandra's role in advancing these causes has earned her respect from both nonprofit organizations and governments.

She has been recognized for her efforts to create a more inclusive society and to help people live with dignity, regardless of their physical or mental challenges. Many groups have praised Sandra for her leadership in supporting social causes that often do not receive enough attention. Sandra's philanthropic work serves as a shining example of how business success can be used to address social issues and create positive change.

Influence in Spain and Worldwide

Sandra Ortega Mera's influence goes beyond the awards she has received. Her impact in Spain, where she is based, has been immense. As the daughter of Amancio Ortega, the founder of Inditex, and a shareholder in the company, Sandra has been able to influence the direction of one of the largest fashion companies in the world. Inditex, which owns Zara and other global fashion brands, has made a significant contribution to the Spanish economy, and Sandra's role in the company has cemented her status as an influential figure in Spain's business world.

Her work at Inditex and other business ventures has also influenced global markets. Sandra's involvement in companies that focus on ethical business practices, sustainability, and social responsibility has made her a leading figure in promoting these values. She has shown that businesses can be successful while also caring for the environment and society. Sandra's leadership has encouraged other business leaders to think about how their actions affect not just profits, but also the people and world around them.

Sandra's influence isn't confined to the boardrooms of Spain. Her impact reaches across the globe, as her work with Inditex and other companies has contributed to global trends in fashion, business practices, and philanthropy. She has helped shape the way people view corporate social responsibility, showing that it is possible to balance making money with doing good for the world.

Inspiration for Women in Business

Sandra Ortega Mera's success story is an inspiration to many, especially to women who aspire to succeed in business. As a woman in a male-dominated industry, Sandra's achievements stand as a powerful reminder that women can succeed in business and leadership roles. Despite coming from a wealthy and influential family, Sandra worked hard to build her own identity in the business world. She did not rely solely on her inheritance, but used her skills, knowledge, and passion to make her mark.

Her journey has encouraged other women to pursue careers in business and to aim for positions of power. Sandra's ability to balance business, philanthropy, and her personal life has shown that women can excel in multiple areas. Her success in managing large companies while also contributing to social causes has broken barriers for women in business and shown that they can lead with integrity and compassion.

Sandra's work also demonstrates the importance of using one's position of influence to support important causes. Many women who look up to Sandra see her as a role model for how to be successful in business while making a meaningful difference in the world. By leading with values and prioritizing social good alongside profits, Sandra has set an example for women who want to make a difference in the business world.

Encouraging Ethical Business Practices

Another aspect of Sandra's recognition is her role in promoting ethical business practices. She has become a leading voice in advocating for businesses to consider the impact of their actions on society and the environment. Sandra's work with Inditex and her investments in companies like PharmaMar demonstrate her commitment to supporting businesses that align with her values.

Sandra has received praise for encouraging companies to adopt sustainable practices and to invest in long-term growth that benefits people, rather than just focusing on short-term profits. Her approach to business is grounded in the belief that companies should play a role in solving social issues, from promoting disability inclusion to supporting environmental sustainability. Sandra's influence has helped shift the way many business leaders think about corporate responsibility, making her a key figure in the movement for more ethical and socially responsible business practices.

A Legacy of Positive Change

Sandra Ortega Mera's recognition in both the business world and the charity sector is a testament to her dedication, hard work, and commitment to positive change. Through her efforts, she has not only contributed to the success of global companies like Inditex but has also made a lasting impact on society. Sandra has shown that business and philanthropy can go hand in hand, and her example continues to inspire others to follow in her footsteps.

Sandra's recognition is not just about awards and honors—it is about the real, lasting impact she has had on the world. Her influence has been felt in Spain, across the business world, and around the globe. As a role model for women in business and a champion of ethical business practices, Sandra Ortega Mera's legacy will continue to inspire future generations of leaders who understand that success should be measured not just by profits, but by the positive difference one can make in the world.

Chapter 9: Sandra's Personal Life and Values

Sandra Ortega Mera, a successful businesswoman and philanthropist, is known for her quiet, family-focused lifestyle. While much of her professional life is public, she has worked hard to keep her personal life private. This chapter explores Sandra's role as a wife and mother, as well as the values that guide her actions both in her personal and professional life.

Sandra's Family Life

Sandra Ortega Mera is a woman who values her family above all else. Despite her significant role in one of the world's largest companies, she has always made time for her family. She is a mother, and her children are an important part of her life. Sandra believes in creating a strong and supportive environment for her family. She is known for her close relationship with her children, and she works hard to make sure they grow up with strong values.

Sandra's family is her top priority. She has always kept her personal life out of the spotlight, choosing to focus on her family rather than seeking public attention. This has allowed her to raise her children in a stable and loving home, away from the pressures and distractions of the media. Sandra's commitment to her family is evident in the way she balances her demanding professional life with her role as a mother.

Her Role as a Wife

Sandra Ortega Mera is also a devoted wife. She has been married for many years and values her relationship with her husband. Sandra's marriage is based on mutual respect, trust, and support. She believes in maintaining a strong partnership and working together as a team to achieve their shared goals. Sandra's relationship with her husband is a key part of her personal life, and they both prioritize their family and their values.

While Sandra is known for her business achievements, her husband plays an important role in her life. Their relationship is one of mutual understanding and collaboration. Sandra has often spoken about how important it is to have a strong support system, and she has been open about how her family, including her husband, has supported her in her various endeavors. This support has allowed Sandra to manage her many responsibilities with confidence and stability.

Balancing Work and Family

One of the most impressive aspects of Sandra Ortega Mera's life is her ability to balance her demanding business career with her family responsibilities. She has managed to build a successful business career while still being a dedicated mother and wife.

Sandra's ability to find balance between her personal and professional life is something many people admire.

She has often said that maintaining this balance is important to her, and she works hard to make sure that neither her family nor her work suffers. Sandra makes sure to spend quality time with her family, even when her business commitments are busy. This includes setting aside time for her children and her husband, and being present for them, whether it is for important events or everyday moments.

Sandra's approach to balancing her career and family life shows that it is possible to be successful in both areas, as long as one remains focused on what truly matters. She has learned to manage her time effectively, and she believes that keeping a clear boundary between work and family life is key to maintaining harmony.

Sandra's Core Values

Sandra Ortega Mera's personal values are a strong foundation for her success. These values guide her decisions both in her personal life and in her business career. Sandra believes in integrity, hard work, and the importance of giving back to society. She is committed to doing the right thing, even when it is not the easiest path.

One of Sandra's most important values is social responsibility. She believes that businesses should contribute to the well-being of society. This belief is reflected in her philanthropic work through Fundación Paideia Galiza, which supports people with disabilities. Sandra believes that everyone should have the opportunity to live a full and dignified life, regardless of their circumstances. Her commitment to helping others is a core value that shapes her personal and professional life.

Sandra also values sustainability and ethical business practices. She has always believed in the importance of businesses acting responsibly and making decisions that have a positive impact on the world. This value is reflected in her involvement with companies like Inditex, which has worked to improve its environmental footprint and promote ethical practices in the fashion industry.

Another value that Sandra holds dear is family. She believes that a strong family bond is essential to living a happy and fulfilling life. Sandra works hard to maintain a close relationship with her children and husband. She believes that family is a source of support and strength, and she makes it a priority to spend time with them.

The Importance of Privacy

Sandra Ortega Mera is known for being a private person. While she is well-known for her business achievements and charitable work, she does not seek the spotlight. Sandra prefers to keep her personal life out of the media, choosing to focus on her family and values rather than public attention. She believes that privacy is important for maintaining balance and peace of mind.

By keeping her personal life private, Sandra is able to create a space where she can be herself and focus on what matters most to her. She has expressed that she values her quiet life and the opportunity to enjoy time with her family without constant public scrutiny. Sandra's approach to privacy has allowed her to protect her family's well-being and maintain a sense of normalcy, despite her high-profile position.

Sandra's choice to keep her personal life private is also a reflection of her desire to maintain control over the narrative of her life. She is not interested in being a public figure for the sake of attention or fame.

Instead, she wants her actions and values to speak for themselves. By focusing on her work and her family, Sandra has built a reputation as a grounded and thoughtful individual who values substance over spectacle.

Sandra's Influence on Others

Despite her preference for privacy, Sandra Ortega Mera's values have had a positive influence on others. Her commitment to family, ethical business practices, and social responsibility serves as an example for others to follow. Sandra has shown that it is possible to be successful in business while staying true to one's values and prioritizing family.

Her work with Fundación Paideia Galiza has inspired others to get involved in charitable causes and to support people with disabilities. Sandra's belief in the importance of giving back has encouraged many individuals and organizations to take action and contribute to their communities. Through her example, Sandra has shown that personal values and professional success can go hand in hand, and that it is possible to live a fulfilling life while making a positive impact on the world.

Sandra Ortega Mera's personal life and values demonstrate that success is not just about achieving professional milestones, but also about living a life that is grounded in principles that matter. Her ability to maintain balance between her family, work, and values has made her a respected figure in both the business world and the community.

Conclusion

Sandra Ortega Mera is a woman who has made a big impact in business and society. Her journey shows how hard work, strong values, and a clear vision can help someone achieve success. From her work with Inditex to her commitment to social causes, Sandra has built a lasting legacy. This chapter reflects on her many accomplishments, her influence, and her continued dedication to making a positive difference in the world.

A Strong Foundation

Sandra's story is one of dedication and perseverance. She began her journey as the daughter of a business tycoon, but she didn't just rely on her inheritance. Instead, she worked hard to build her own path. Sandra's involvement in businesses like Inditex, the company behind Zara, has allowed her to become a major figure in the global business world. Through her work, she has shown that it is possible to take a family business and turn it into something bigger and better while maintaining the company's values.

Sandra didn't just focus on growing the business for herself. She believed in using her position to help others. One of her greatest achievements has been her commitment to social causes, particularly those related to people with disabilities. Through Fundación Paideia Galiza, Sandra has worked to provide opportunities and support for people who face challenges in life. Her work in this area has helped many individuals and has set an example for other business leaders to follow.

Sandra's journey is not just about business success. It is about creating a legacy that will last long after she is gone. She has proven that it is possible to make a significant impact on the world, not just by building wealth but by making the world a better place for others.

Making a Difference in Business

In business, Sandra Ortega Mera is a role model. She has shown that you don't have to be in the spotlight to be influential. While many business leaders seek fame and attention, Sandra prefers to focus on the work itself. Her leadership has been key to the growth of Inditex, which has become one of the largest fashion retailers in the world. But her success isn't just measured in numbers or sales. It is measured by the positive influence she has had on the way businesses can operate responsibly.

Sandra's approach to business is built on ethical practices and social responsibility. She has used her position to encourage companies to consider their impact on the environment, their workers, and the communities they serve. Sandra understands that businesses are not just about profits; they are about people. This belief has led her to support many initiatives that promote sustainability and ethical business practices.

Sandra's influence extends beyond Inditex. She has become a symbol of responsible business leadership. Her success shows that it is possible to build a company that is both profitable and socially responsible. Many people admire her ability to balance the needs of a business with the needs of society. Sandra's work has inspired other entrepreneurs to think about how they can use their businesses to make the world a better place.

A Commitment to Social Impact

Sandra Ortega Mera's philanthropic work is one of the most important aspects of her legacy. She has spent many years supporting social causes, particularly those related to people with disabilities. Through Fundación

Paideia Galiza, Sandra has helped create programs that provide support, education, and employment opportunities for people who often face discrimination. She believes that everyone deserves a chance to succeed, regardless of their background or abilities.

Sandra's commitment to social causes is not just about giving money or support; it is about making lasting change. She has used her position and influence to bring attention to important social issues. Sandra believes that businesses and individuals alike have a responsibility to give back to society. Her work in this area has had a significant impact on many lives and continues to inspire others to get involved in charitable causes.

In addition to her work with Fundación Paideia Galiza, Sandra has supported other initiatives that promote education, healthcare, and sustainability. She understands that the world faces many challenges, and she is determined to do her part in addressing them. Sandra's work shows that one person, no matter how successful, can make a huge difference in the world.

Legacy of Leadership

Sandra Ortega Mera's legacy is built on her leadership, her commitment to making a difference, and her ability to inspire others. She has shown that true success is not just about personal achievement but about how one can help others and make the world a better place. Sandra's influence goes beyond the business world; it extends into the fields of charity, social responsibility, and sustainability.

Her leadership has been a model for other women in business. Sandra has demonstrated that women can be just as successful as men in business and that they can do so while maintaining their values and making a positive impact on society. She has proven that it is possible to be both a strong business leader and a compassionate individual who cares about the world around her.

Sandra's work has inspired many people, especially women, to pursue their dreams and create positive change. She has shown that you don't have to choose between success and social responsibility—you can have both. Sandra's legacy will continue to inspire future generations of business leaders and philanthropists to make a difference in their communities and the world.

Continuing the Journey

Sandra Ortega Mera's journey is far from over. While she has already achieved so much, she remains dedicated to making a positive impact. Her work with Fundación Paideia Galiza continues to help people with disabilities, and her commitment to ethical business practices has influenced many other companies around the world. Sandra's dedication to social responsibility and sustainability remains strong, and she is always looking for new ways to create lasting change.

As she continues her work, Sandra's influence will only grow. She has shown that success is not just about financial achievement; it is about making a difference. Her journey is an example of how one person can have a lasting impact on the world. Through her work, Sandra Ortega Mera has created a legacy that will inspire future generations to be leaders, to care for others, and to make the world a better place.

In conclusion, Sandra Ortega Mera's story is one of hard work, dedication, and making a difference. From her achievements in business to her contributions to social causes, she has created a legacy that will inspire others for many years to come. Sandra's commitment to responsible business practices, philanthropy, and social responsibility shows that success is not just about profits, but about how we use our success to make a positive impact on the world.